Prize-wir
Nation<

Contents

Foreword	3
Introduction	4
View From the Beach	6
Natural World	10
The Unsaved Place	21
Think Global	33
Bricks and Mortar	46
Trust Us	56
Index	63

**The National Trust
1895–1995**

Special thanks are due to:

- The Vivien Duffield Foundation for supporting the competition and the production of this anthology.

- Eureka!, The Museum for Children, in Halifax, West Yorkshire, for hosting the prize giving on 15 November 1995.

- All the judges, for undertaking the daunting task of selecting the winning poems from 14,000 entries.

- And, most importantly, all the children and schools – prize winners and non-prize winners – who sent in their **Saving Places** poems.

First published in 1996 by National Trust (Enterprises) Ltd.,
36 Queen Anne's Gate, London SW1H 9AS
Registered Charity No. 205846

© text and cover illustration The National Trust 1996
The moral rights of the authors have been asserted.

All rights reserved. No part of this publications may be reproduced, stored in a retrieval system or transmitted by any means, electronic, mechanical, photocopying or otherwise, without the prior permission of the publisher.

ISBN 0-7078-0276-8

Edited by Sally Bacon
Designed and produced by Vivitext Creative Services,
Printed by Whitstable Litho Printers, Whitstable, Kent.

Foreword from the judges

It is often said that trying to judge poems is an impossibility because it is so subjective. Well, yes and no.

The Saving Places judges met one mild autumn day on the top floor of the Trust's London headquarters. Outside, the sun was shining in St. James's Park and I think we all wondered if we would become embroiled in arguments over the merits of one poem against another. We each write in very different ways and we privately dreaded finding that the others would not agree with our personal shortlists. But it did not happen like that.

We had all found the poems to be of a high standard and very enjoyable. And, what's more, we discovered a remarkable measure of agreement between our shortlists. As we compared notes we revelled in the varied approaches and appreciated the technical ability of many of the entrants. Favourite poems and phrases were read out and savoured. We felt completely positive about, and, at times, humbled by, the talent of these young writers and all agreed that it was possibly the most enjoyable judging session we had ever taken part in.

So much for it being impossible to judge poetry. When three very different writers independently select the same poems, there must be some common standard applied by each of them. The subjective element comes really at the final stage. When poems are considered equally good, but are in different forms and by young writers of quite different ages, it is virtually impossible to choose who should come first. Again, we were in complete agreement that in two age categories we wanted joint winners. So that is how it was.

We were delighted to judge this competition and felt privileged to read the work of so many children who not only care about saving places, but also about language and poetry.

Sandy Brownjohn
Gillian Clarke
Roger McGough

Tony Robinson was Special Guest Judge.
Elin ap Hywel was the judge of the Welsh language category (winner on p.19).

Introduction

For the National Trust's centenary celebrations in 1995, it was important that young people – and the next 100 years – should be placed centre stage. Events and special happenings were planned for children at hundreds of properties – but how could the National Trust provide something more permanent, that would still be around long after the events and celebrations had ended?

Young people throughout Britain were invited to show, through poetry, why saving their environment was important to them. A poetry competition would not only give the National Trust a chance to hear their views on its work, but also provide a lasting, collective statement of their vision of its past, present and future.

And that is exactly what this anthology represents; 14,000 young writers answered the Trust's challenge, and, in doing so, articulated what the Trust, in all its richness and diversity, is essentially all about.

All the writers published here were aged between 5 and 15 when they wrote their poems. Work was submitted in different age categories; 8 and under, 9 to 12 and 13 to15, although we have published the ages of the poets at the time of the announcement of the winners, not the time of writing. There are 10 overall winning poems, including the winner in the Welsh language category, and 45 runners-up.

In collecting these poems together for publication, we have grouped them by subject matter rather than by age. This proved quite a task, as so many of the writers had woven a complex web of different ideas – a testament to their commitment to, and knowledge of, the issues they were writing about. However, the final categories reflect the final breakdown of main themes among all the poems entered, as well as the chief concerns voiced by the winners and runners-up.

Beginning with the very edges of Britain, **View From The Beach** brings together the poems which take the coastline as their starting point – its cliffs and bays, its inhabitants, its buildings, and the power of the sea. The section begins with a poem from our youngest entrant about people saving buildings – lighthouses – which in turn save people.

Introduction

By far the most popular topic was the **Natural World.** Many poems recorded its beauty and importance; many also mourned its gradual destruction. Here are the poems which focus on the beauty to be found in all natural forms, whilst hinting at the threats posed to them. A bleaker view is taken by the poems in the section called **The Unsaved Place**, which is also the title of the poem by Thomas O'Rourke (11). These poems offer readers a grim ultimatum – a picture of a world in which, unless we take action, nature is destroyed and the bulldozers take over.

Next comes **Think Global**, which looks not just at issues such as protecting rain forests, but also at attitudes to the environment, and its conservation. As many of the poets tell us, conservation is actually about people – our thoughts, lifestyles, actions and approaches to our responsibilities.

But the natural environment was not the only topic covered – as Brigid Jones (8) noted, the National Trust is also the 'Doctor of Castles'. **Bricks and Mortar** leads readers to another dimension of saving places – protecting the built environment for people to enjoy.

And finally, **Trust Us**. This is a book about saving places – not their destruction – but some of the poets tell us that we must sometimes look first at the 'unsaved place', to see the consequences of human actions and apathy, before we can determine the right course of action. With **Trust Us**, the collection ends on a note of optimism, and looks ahead to the Trust's second century with some glimpses of what is to be done – by individuals, by the Trust, and by others. It is this optimism which underpins the whole collection.

On 15 November 1995, the winners were invited to Eureka!, The Museum for Children, West Yorkshire, to receive their prizes from actor and special guest judge, Tony Robinson. For the Trust, and, we hope, for all the winners and entrants, this book is the best prize of all.

Sally Bacon
Saving Places Co-ordinator

View From the Beach

Lighthouse

Shaped like a lipstick
with white and red stripes.
Found by the sea.
To keep ships away from the rocks
light bright as the moon
flashes like lightning.
In the foggy gloom
a voice like a trumpet
calls "Keep Away!", "Keep Away!".
We should save lighthouses
because lighthouses save lives.

James Winterbourne (5)*

View From the Beach

Saving Kimmeridge Bay, Dorset

I like the cracking, crumbling cliffs,
The glorious sky,
And the furious sea.
The oily shale that smells when you break it,
The shiny seaweed that smells when you shake it.

I like the glimmering shimmering rock pools,
The racy shrimps,
And the lacy fish.
The anenomes that cling to your fingers,
The curious crabs that nibble your fingers.

I like the shells that cover the seashore,
The crinkly cockles,
And the wrinkly whelks.
The barnacles bristling on slate on the seabed,
The limpets that stick to the rocks on the seabed.

I like the fossils preserved over centuries,
The curl of their shape,
And the squirl of their shells
The fragile fossils that flake if you tap them,
The delicate fossils that snap if you touch them.

I like the colourful boats in the bay,
The lazy sea breeze,
And the hazy sea sun,
The fisherman sitting at work on the shoreline,
The yachts out at sea silhouetting the skyline.

I would like Kimmeridge kept safe for my children,
No drilling for oil,
No killing sea life
Keep Kimmeridge protected from deadly pollution
Keep Kimmeridge protected from man's evolution.

Rachel Jones (9)*

Freedom To Oblivion

A howling voice trapped in the wind
Flies, yelling, across the stony sands.
White foam, like liquid air, crests wave-tops
And the grassy dunes give up their height
To the unseen force in this unpeopled place.
And to the left looking out to sea
Tall giants stand frozen from some ancient curse
But men now call them cliffs.
So, on this day the clouds stroll past
Like curtains covering the window like sky.
Pounding fists thump the giants' feet,
Crying for some vengeance unthought of,
Undiscovered by humankind but known to nature.
For a thousand years this craggy creation
Has held the secret of the mysterious balance of existence.

The angry winds are no hindrance
To the Lords of the Sky.
With their great winged arms outstretched
Only they know the ecstasy of flight.
Falling, but still called soaring, in a way,
Is the gull from its abode in the cliff.
She caws a harsh guttural sound
As a warning unheard and unheeded.
The glassy boundary of the sea comes ever closer
Until the spring is released and then
Smoothly down, then up with a fish:
This is nature's balance.

The flash comes and the sea is dark and strange.
Dunes are gone and stone, unlike the giants', replaces it.
A torrent of animal killers, men, come running
With noise and metal beasts of destruction.
Fish, gull and creature can be no more.

Reuben Rowe (13)

Dunwich

My first view of the sea was from the cliff top.
Calm and blue,
The white waves slowly curving over,
And sliding up the beach
Leaving swervy patterns behind on the sand.

Down on the shingle beach,
The waves came slithering up to my toes,
Leaving white foam clinging to my shoes,
Then scratching back over the stones.
Pebbles were left behind, smooth and shiny,
Water trickling back into the blue expanse of sea.

Is this the same sea
That came to Dunwich cliff?
Violent, crashing waves,
Roaring and raging,
Eating and swallowing a town.

Thundering breakers collapsing cliffs,
Battering and bullying, punching and pounding;
All a terrible tragedy.
Not a bit like my view of Dunwich;
Calm and blue
So the sea seemed.

Johnnie Sims (9)

Natural World

Separation

Here lies a rock – well, it's really a pebble,
Kicked aside as the children paddle:
Smooth and glazed with silvery gleam
Given to it by the rushing stream,
Grey on the underside, streaked with red
From iron deposits on the river bed.
I reach out and lift it from the waters
But as I do, the beauty falters:
The red-gold iron no longer glows
And the silver sheen no longer shows.
It's diminished in size to a dull grey stone –
Worthless, lying here on its own.
I step to the bank now and let it go –
Slip it back into the water's flow
And see the gentle transformation
As it finds what was lost during separation.

Keren White (14)*

Natural World

Owl-Girl

The black, still night ...
People stir in their sleep.
The leaves from a weary tree
Fall right to the root of the trunk.
A cold wind blows, lightly,
Leaving behind its unsettled peace.
The trees stand tall,
But the earth still shakes beneath them
Because there is sadness ...
Where a girl walks on the leaves,
Crackles on the sodden forest floor.
She takes a breath of clear air.
Slowly, brown, long feathers cover her arms.
Eyes change to a sparkle of dark black.
The moon reflects in her new eyes
And Owl-Girl
Flies toward the moon
And whispers ...
"I am the Guardian of the forests,
The protector of the trees."
A single feather falls ...
And lands,
Covered by the silent leaves.

Kim Craven (13)

Natural World

Foxes

Chestnut coats,
Sleek black legs:
The foxes creep through the night.
Melting shadows,
Sleepless pitch:
Through the darkness and out of sight.

Then the horn sounds:
The hounds bay,
The fox starts to run:
Run, run-away!

Run through the valleys,
And over the hills,
And across the springs,
Where rivers fill.

Will this fox make it;
Or will she die?
Out in a field,
Her body shall lie.

Torn and scattered,
Here and there,
But don't they see?
Do they care?

The fox they have killed;
She'll lie and lie.
Not an ear for an ear,
Nor an eye for an eye.

Just another life lost –
Killed like a fly.
But why do they do it?
WHY, WHY, WHY?

Katy Bagshaw (12)

Natural World

A Poem Of Preservation

Put a preservation order on this tree –
Recognise its value; it's not just for me.
Everything in it; each branch and each leaf
Should be respected. That's my belief.
Every creature on this earth
Relies upon this tree from birth.
Vital gifts like healthy air
And homes for many, sheltered there,
This tree provides, and also shade.
In ancient beauty which God made.
One brutal axe could fell this tree
Never harm it; it stands so free.

Sarah Berkson (11)

Natural World

The Dream Of the Oak Tree

The oak tree dreams,
Rocked into troubled sleep
By the movement of the wind
In her branches.

In her sleep, she dreams ...
Of times past and future.
For a tree's memory is huge.

She dreams of the war,
That dreadful day
When an aircraft burst into flames
On the neighbours' lawn.
And the pilot came floating down,
Wounded, mortally.

But now, in her slumber,
The falling pilot is a sapling
Which she watched slowly growing ...
From an acorn, borne by her boughs.

Now she lets her dreams wander,
And wonder ...
How many years before she is brought down?
How will she fall?

But now her dreams flicker,
Like an old film.
And leave her to battle the wind.

And ...
During her dreams
The winds picks up,
And she is dancing ...
A drunken ballerina
Trying to waltz.

Robert Goss (13)*

Natural World

A Swan Is On The Water

A swan is on the water;
It looks like another swan is stuck to its feet under water.
It is daytime, so the sun can make another swan.
Then, the wind ripples the water
And the reflection is wavy.
Straight lines of grasses at the edge
Are crinkly lines in the mirror of the water;
But it wasn't always like that ...

Cans and bottles floated on brown sludge,
Nothing could live there,
A black slime on the surface of the water,
And nobody cared.

But now, someone does care,
The pond is clean,
Ducks nest around its grassy edges,
And swans can paddle around
And look at their faces in the water.

Rhys Grant (7)

The Wood is Alive

The wood is alive
The trees are breathing
The sunlight shines through the trees
Lighting up the floor.

The squirrels playfully run up trees
And hide from me
The rabbits run to and fro
It's nice to see them play.

Sometimes I see a deer
They are very shy
Must be quiet
Or it will run away.

The birds sing in the trees
Some chirp and some caw
It's really nice to hear them
They are a natural orchestra.

Sometimes if you come here early
You can see and hear night-time creatures
The wood is home to many animals
That is why it is important to look after it.

Bethany Knight (6)

Natural World

Save Our Weeds

When is a weed not a weed?
I'd really like to know.
You don't exactly sow them,
They just seem to grow.

Take a look at a nettle,
(It has another name),
And I think you'll agree,
It really isn't the same.
A beautiful shade of yellow,
It can be pink or white
And when you go to pick it,
It hasn't that awful bite!

He's broad of leaf
And strong in stem
We tend to get a lot of them
Now Dr. Dock is just the thing
To take away the nettle's sting.

Flea bane, Sneezewort and Ragwort
Hairy violet, Radish and Rocket,
Are hardly the kind of plants
You'd happily put in your pocket.

There's a monster who lives by the river
The very thought of him makes me shiver
He's the Giant Hog weed,
And he'll eat you alive
Brains, heart, lungs, kidney and liver.

But butterflies and lady birds
Dragon flies and bees,
Come from miles and miles away
To get a sniff of these.
So in your garden, please keep a place
For the weed who is only a plant out of place.

Hugo Bourne (8)

Natural World

The Best Place

My grandma took me for a walk
to the best place I have been,
We saw big tall mountains
and paddled in a stream.

My Gran showed me a bird's nest
high up in a tree,
We didn't try to touch it
It's full of eggs you see.

We sat and had a picnic on grass
So soft and green,
It was very quiet
In this best place I have ever been.

My Gran says it's a special place
Made by God in Heaven,
I hope that it's still here when
My kids are aged seven.

Gavin Rowley (8)

Cors Caron

I deithiwr sy'n gwibio yn ei gar,
dwyt ti'n ddim ond cors lwyd, farw!
Ni wel y bywyd sy'n llifo drwot ti
wrth i Deifi nadreddu ei ffordd
drwy'r mawn.

Ynot ti mae hud y canrifoedd,
a swyn hen chwedlau'n suo'n dawel
wrth i'r gwynt ddweud ei stori
yn yr hesg.

Sisial mae Teifi ei hanes hen
a chanu ymysg y brwyn i'r adar mân,
wrth i geiliog y rhedyn sgrechen ei dôn
ar ddydd o haf.

Uwchben mae'r boda fforch-gynffon
a'i gri ddolefus fel baban mewn poen,
wrth i'r brain grawcio'n sbeitlyd arno
a'i regi'n ddibaid.

I deithiwr sy'n gwibio yn ei gar,
dwyt ti'n ddim ond cors lwyd, farw!
I minnau mae llawennydd dy gwmni'n fy llonni
A chleber Teifi a Brennig
Yn llanw fy mryd.

Llywelyn Evans (12)*

...garon Bog

To the traveller, zooming past in his car,
you're nothing but a dead grey bog!
He doesn't see the life flowing through you
as the Teifi snakes its way
through the peat.

The magic of centuries is in you,
the enchantment of old legends, whispering quietly
as the wind in the sedges tells its tale.

Teifi murmurs its old story,
singing to the small birds among the rushes,
as the grasshopper screeches his song
on a summer's day.

Above, the fork-tailed kite's
mournful cry is like a baby in pain,
as the crows croak spitefully at him,
swearing incessantly.

To the traveller, zooming past in his car,
you're nothing but a dead grey bog!
To me the pleasure of your company is a joy
and the chatter of Teifi and Brennig
fill me with delight.

*Llywelyn Evans (12)**

Translated from the Welsh by Elin ap Hywel

The Unsaved Place

The unsaved place is
A place of death.
The unsaved place
is a deserted place.
The unsaved place is
Where the sun doesn't shine.
The unsaved place is at
The end of the line.

Thomas O'Rourke (12)

We Are The Bulldozers

We are the bulldozers
And our blades can demolish a town;
We are the strongest, the fiercest and best,
We are monsters of ruin.
We chew up your meadows and taste the grass,
Our teeth are sharp and made of shiny silver,
People think they own us,
But we can tear down your past
To build our future!
We'd dig up the Universe if we could,
    flatten fields, break buildings,
    uproot and undermine,
    devastate and destroy,
    wreck and ruin,
We are out of your control,
For we are the bulldozers!

Sarah Sillett (10)

The Unsaved Place

Saving Places

This is where the oak trees stood
The men came in to cut them down
We protested, but they said,
 "We can, we will"
 "We could, we would"
We said "No, no that's not the way,
Just you listen to what we say"
 We said
 "Stop, stop ... please."

This is where the oak trees stood,
The men came in, to cut them down,
We protested, but they said
 "We can, we will."
 They could, They would
 and
 They did.

You can hear the echoes of lifeless branches
The crackle of dead wood underfoot
 They could
 They would
 They did.

Katherine Eley (12)

The Unsaved Place

Ten Healthy Woodlands

Ten healthy woodlands standing in a line.
One gets cleared for a housing estate.
Then there were nine.
Nine peaceful woodlands grieving the other one's fate.
One gets chopped down for fire wood.
Then there were eight.
Eight wet woodlands looking up at heaven.
One gets infected with acid rain.
Then there were seven.
Seven mischievous woodlands shedding some sticks.
Someone flicks a cigarette.
Then there were six.
Six cheerful woodlands happy to be alive.
One is chopped down for farmland.
Then there were five.
Five tired woodlands beginning to snore.
One is chopped down for paper.
Then there were four.
Four miserable woodlands standing in a melee.
One gets uprooted for excavation.
Then there were three.
Three cold woodlands one with the flu.
Finds out it has a fungus.
Then there were two.
Two unhappy woodlands one very old with depression
Someone gives it a kick
Then there was one.
One lonely woodland getting warmed by the sun.
Gets too hot and lonely
Then there were NONE.

Sarah Cam (11)

The River

The deep holes of cows' hooves
Make ruts
As I jump to and from,
Skipping and hopping to ...

The river
Which swirls its way along the field,
Like a thread on a carpet.
The steep edges end, abruptly,
Like little cliffs.

And the stones,
Coated in a green, dull varnish,
Roll slowly down the river ...

Where the fish weave
In and out of the stones,
Jumping like fleas.
And as their thin bodies twitch,
I try to catch them.

Down the river,
Fresh water mussels
Hide beneath the mud,
Their shells like ...

Two spoons,
Which have lost their handles,
Tightly glued together
And spotted along the water,
Like Dalmatians' fur.

It's changed now.
They put in a sewage pipe.
They made the stones black.
The fish float
And mussels open and die.
Is this my river?

May Camplin (13)

The Unsaved Place

The Wild Side

There's a place.
Just south of the garden fence and about seven
 steps to the left.
Through the willow trees
down beneath the reeds and the poppies
The stream almost "bubbles"
Our names carved on the tree above our heads.
"I love so and so." "Thingumybob 4 me."
 "True love forever"
Memories, almost embarrassing
If you sit there, the tree wraps itself around you,
 like a big armchair. Familiar
the slight knobble that gives you a backache
 if you sit there for long enough.
Down to the right of the reeds there's a stone,
 which punctured my skin when I was
 six after a game of "It."
The scar is still there, just above the left kneecap.
And there just under the fence, there's a bramble
 patch which we used to throw our brothers'
 clothes in after skinny dipping.
The large oak which my friend Sarah fell from and
 broke her leg.
She never came again.
The wild side we called it.
I remember the nights we snuck out – clambering
 out of the bedroom window.
Searching for werewolves, or ghouls or ghosts
 or something.
I remember the excitement.
The times I crept out to meet David or Graham
 or Simon or Jamie. So romantic.
A quick kiss and a cuddle after dark.

The Unsaved Place

I remember sitting there under the stars among the
   trees and the water.
But it was more than just trees and water.
It was the wild side
It's like a piece of me – a special part of me.
And now it's going the sound of the bulldozers and
   cement mixers ring in my ears.
It's going and I'm going. Goodbye wild side. If only
   I could keep you, preserve you
for someone else to enjoy you as much as I did.
And now as I get up to leave it almost feels as if I'm
   saying goodbye to an old friend.

Alissa Barlow (age 14)

The Unsaved Place

When it all Changed

First came the woodcutters cutting down the trees.
Then came the workmen building the road.
Then came the builders building houses.
Then came the people moving into their homes.
Then came the supermarkets
Asda, Sainsburys, Tesco and Safeways
Then came the fumes that came from
The cars that came from the people
That live in the houses
That are by the road
That was built by the workmen
Who used the wood from trees
That the woodcutter cut down.

Louise Stockton (8)

A Secret Place

Rain falls gently
On the surface of the pond.
Bees land silently
On open flowers.
A bird sings its song of freedom
From a treetop.
Cow parsley lies in soft flurries
Along the lane.

But in the distance
Smoke rises,
Traffic zooms,
A plane cuts across the open sky.

How long before
even this secret place is invaded?

Eleanor Gilbert (8)

The Last Squirrel

There was once a wood
Where dead trees stood,
Where the bats hung down like the devil's
    decorations
And branches twisted and tangled like uncut hair.
Trees were crusted with moss,
Ancient hieroglyphics of an old race.

There was once a wood
Where eyes peered from the black hearts of dead
    trees,
And the light shone through the branches,
Creating a slithering, snapping monster,
With blood from the dark side of the moon.
A monster trapped in this cage of trees,
Where the last squirrel jumped to the last branch,
Only to find that it snapped like brittle bone.

Adam Stanborough (13)

Saving Places

O squirrel, O squirrel, O squirrel in that tree,
Why don't you ever start looking at me?
With your bushy tail and your fluffy paws
You use the ground not a chest of drawers.
Are you a friend of the butterflies bright?
Are your colours dark or light?
When the day has finished you go to hide
'Til the next time the sun will rise.

O squirrel, O squirrel, O squirrel in that tree,
Pollution on the land and pollution in the sea.
Why do the trees have to be cut down
to make cities and houses in the town?
The world should be safe for us all to live.
We must learn to live together and learn to forgive.
We must look after the world and show we care
So it's safe for the future and everyone to share.

Sarah Graham (7)

Save Our Living Forests

Don't chop down our forests
Please don't, please.
Don't chop down our living forests
Or destroy our ancient trees.

Sly old foxes live in holes,
With their bushy, ginger tails
Raise their fox cubs in our forests
And our woody hills and dales.

Bouncy bob-tailed rabbits hop.
And owls hunt their prey.
Squirrels scamper up the trees,
With twigs to build their dray.

Ponds with cascading waterfalls,
And silvery diving fish,
Are hidden deep in forests
Where the swaying rushes swish.

Tall trees stretch up to the skies,
With gnarled brown crusty bark
Their thick branches block the sunlight
Make our forests midnight dark.

Our forests are a precious place
We must save them from destruction,
And fight to keep our forests green
Not lose them to construction.

Katharine Jones (8)

The Unsaved Place

The Pond

Concrete jungles rising,
Through the murky air.
Man's evil plot is thickening –
What have you done Man?
Dropped a bomb on nature!
Your greed is widening –
You shall not have my pond!
My dove of peace –
Where the swan resides,
Grooming itself,
Gracefully,
Calmly,
Where the reeds stand up with wet feet,
Foxgloves tinkle their bells.
Seedheads of the dandelion clocks
Fall around like silken parachutes.
Stickleback can't be seen.
Hiding amongst the gravel and rocks
Where the sun doesn't shine.
Up above the sun shines upon the water,
I say goodbye and walk through clouds of trees.

Gillian Moore (10)

The Unsaved Place

Saving Places

Brede Valley would be lost
if we had a bypass here.
Even just one road would mess it up.
The food for the sheep would be polluted
and it would ruin the fields.
At night the bright light of the moon and the stars
would not show up
for car lights would shine bright too.

I like the Brede Valley
the sheep dung
the fresh air
the wide open spaces
and the slow flowing rivers
which twist and turn round the bendy banks
where very tall reeds grow
and where swans paddle through the water
trying not to hit a pipe or another swan
as they paddle through the duckweed.

Luciano Frige (9)

Bleeding Green

"Save the world" said the man in the coat,
As I passed him by in my little round car.
I rolled down my window and took the printed paper.
It writhed in my hands and then I heard them, my trees were crying,
Their shuddering sobs were seeping through the sheet,
Their blood trickling over the ink.
Weeping for their friends, weeping for their enemies.
Counting the minutes, the hours, the days.
Clenching and unclenching their soft, green fists,
Trembling with fear at every blustery breath.
"Save the forests" said the man in the coat,
Shaking his bucket, the coins echoed and ricocheted off rubber walls.
Pouring my heart into that well, I thought of all the green that I loved.
The green I'd frolicked in, on long, hot days.
Green that we hung the washing out to dry on.
Green that licked the paving stones, oozing between the cracks.
Green seas with billowing grasses, clans of violets, and furry red caterpillars.
All that vast amount of green, the skin of the earth, depended on me.
Me and my coins,
That flashed and danced and slithered downwards
Meeting the bottom with a metallic slap
Which would trample the axes with lumbering feet,
They would flatten the chainsaws with great, sweeping arms.

Think Global

My coins would save perhaps one tree from a raw,
 savage death.
Then it would grow under the protection of an
 invisible, impenetrable bubble,
That would shut out the timber yards,
The building contractors, the highway constructors,
The rich skyscraper corporations,
Who strip and tear and scratch away and waste
The emerald jewels that sustain each breath we take.
"Save the trees" said the man in the coat;
To me, he smiled and with his eyes said "Thank You".

Sophie Mills (15)*

Saving Places

Speed of life, fast.
It's like walkin' barefoot over broken glass,
It's like jumping rope on a razor blade,
All lightning quick decisions are made,
Lifestyle plush, females rush,
The high profile personality, who earns his pay
 illegally.
Professional liar, school boys admire,
Young girls desire, very few live to retire,
Cash flow EXTREME, dress code supreme, vocabulary
 OBSCENE,
DEFINITION – saving places,
You know what I mean
A PLACE worth going to IS A PLACE worth SAVING.

Kelly Anderson (14)

Suburbia Revisited

Cruising through the city streets
I'm floating in a dreamy daze:
Different sights in different places
Astound, delight, confuse, amaze.

These perfect homes with pretty flowers
Seem normal – am I still alive?
A chic interior inspires revulsion
But decorative falseness seems to thrive.

Posh nosh translates as pangs of hunger
Shag pile means "take off your shoes"
A downstairs loo, an en suite shower –
From status symbols you pick and choose.

I'm walking round in disbelief
Staring at niceness and primness and twee
Where's the reality? Where's all the litter?
This ain't no paradise – it's hell for me:

I'm yearning for fag ends worn into the pavement
And fly posters stuck on all the street's lights
Cars without windows and children with nose rings,
Joy riding, drug abuse, muggings and fights.

That's what this city is actually like,
With ten storey tower blocks breeding young thugs
And windows with bars on and bars without windows
Not love and companionship, friendship and hugs.

Why then a difference in only one mile:
What make this area better than that?
The sense of community? The pleasant front gardens?
The large brand new cars? The pedigree cats?

Or is it just money, the point in society
Where once similar people are divided in two.
The rich and the poor: the problem is obvious,
But where's the solution – what can we do?

Christopher Landau (15)

Think Global

Jungle Poem

All of my crocodiles, swimming log-like down the swirling river looking for food.
All of my monkeys, swinging one-handed through the trees, never touching the ground.
All of my tigers looking hungrily from the shadows, to watch for their food approaching.
All of my snakes slithering across the jungle floor.
All of my huge trees, pushing their branches, spreading giant leaves.
All of my insects, hiding in holes in the trees, tiny biting monsters.
All of my panthers, hiding in the long grass when people come to disturb the jungle peace.
All of my parrots, heard but not seen, hiding in a great big tree, their green home.
All of my jaguars stretched out on branches.
All of my elephants walking in this jungle all day – they are noisy thunderous living bulldozers.
All of my jungle is hot and wet for the animals that make their home there and that is how they like it.

Cassandra Chilvers (8)

Too Late

We've been somewhere great today
We stopped at mega-bite on the way
I've never seen anything like in the whole of 2010
And I know I won't see anything like it again
It's a machine so wonderful you wouldn't believe
No wonder people don't want to leave
After seeing this thing and all it can do
I was amazed and you would be too.

It takes in bad gasses and expels good
And absorbs sunlight into its green hood
It helps the soil under the ground
There isn't another one to be found
People flock from near or far
By sonic rail or old fashioned car.

There are marvellous stories to be told
Passed on to the young from the old
Of when these machines were everywhere to be found
In every village, every city, every town
It was in the 1990's that they began to die
And no-one can really tell us why
People say they didn't know how
But they didn't save them and they regret it now.

If I'd been alive then and it was up to me
I would have saved the machine called a "tree".

Jo Benfield (14)

Think Global

Saving Places – I Thought I Saw

I thought I saw a fertile plain
Growing a crop of golden corn.
I thought I saw the sea again but –
It's probably just the light of dawn.

I thought I saw the proud Elephant
Patrolling by the lake.
I thought I saw the boxing kangaroo but –
It must have been a mistake.

I thought I saw the mighty buffalo,
Stampeding through the forest.
I thought I saw a modest honey bee but –
It could not have been – I promise.

I thought I saw the arrogant kingfisher,
Flashing his red-orange chest.
I thought I saw a bounding hare but –
Maybe my eyes just need a rest.

All these things –
They could not be
They all died out because of me.

Hannah Tobin (10)

Think Global

Earth

If you look into the sun-dried bracken,
Swirled into patterns,
(Curled and twisted into the indecipherable script
Of the Great One who guards the heath),
Down into the undiscovered hole of mist,
Where time is coiled and compressed
Into his mysterious breath ...
If you look down below the line in the rock
Where ice-old ancestors built fires
And worshipped the Great One ...
If you look down into that place,
Deep into the vapour of time,
You will find one solitary tree,
Congested by roads, houses, factories,
Clogging the air with a thick grey fog.
And on the tree will be a man
Who tries to feed his own oily face.
Then you will see the past, the wilderness.
And man himself will be there, content with life,
Feeding everything but his own unblemished face.
And then the Great One himself,
In all his beauty, all in a glow,
Brighter than the sun itself,
Will ask you which of these places you want.
Only one is the future
Only you can decide.

Henry Thomas (13)

Think Global

Rain Forest

This can go next –
Here let me draw the line,
That's roughly right,
Give or take a few miles or so,
I'll list the new ones we need,
No burn the rest
Only take the best,
We're not in this for charity,
Replant? No –
You're new to this, I see,
There's plenty more where that came from,
No problem! Finish here and then move on ...

The butterflies are blinded by smoke,
Then drift like torn paper to the flames below ...
The sun sinks behind the high canopy,
The iron men are silenced,
The moon rises,
The fire fly wakes,
Death pauses for a night ...
Spider, last of her kind,
Scuttles underground, safe,
Prepares her nest for young ones,
But none come ...
They have stolen my land,
The birds have flown,
The people gone,
The rainbow rises over sand,
The river flows over stone ...
The land has gone,
The people have flown,
The sun scorches our earth,
The river weeps ...

Nina Whitford (15)

Saving Places

So fast, can't stop ...
Bung it in the microwave,
Wait for the toast to click and take a phone call,
Slap it on the plate,
Run for the tube.

No time to muck about.
No time to look.
No time to care?

The dry stone wall stands still,
Multicoloured, warm and comfortable,
Did it look like this last year?
Or the year before that?

Change comes slowly to an old stone wall.
No one alive is so old or so permanent.

Will my children rush around like me?
They will run out of time too?
Will they, like me, love that old, old wall?
Will it still be there and is it up to me?
IT HAD BETTER BE!

Cecilia Murphy (9)

Think Global

The Gareloch

The gulls swoop down on Gareloch's shore, and screech.
Bare barren rocks, no seaweed, nothing fit to eat.
The fern, the bracken, heather, firs, all doomed,
And in their place, barbed fences guard the concrete, fortressed tomb.

There's some who say deterrents are a must.
Bigger and better bombs, annihilation, death, destruction. Worse.
I don't agree, I do not like war games,
The next time will be Armageddon, the Apocalypse.

Dark and menacing, a submarine slips out to sea,
Can no one see what is in store, but me.
I turn away. I canna see for tears.
How long is left. Do others share my fears?

The Gareloch, Benbecula, Loch Long, Glen Fruin.
Now chilling, formidable, desolate. Ruined.
But ...
What's this I see, through the fence, by the Ben.
Tall, proud and majestic, alone in the Glen.

A thistle
Our emblem.
Symbolic?
Amen.

Ciara McKeown (16)*

Think Global

Saving Places

I know a place,
So silent and still,
I know a place,
Where fresh waters spill,
Down from the rocks like silver and gold,
Tumbling free, so strong and so bold.

I know a place,
Where fairy tales live,
I know a place,
That still knows how to give,
Dreams for the future made of hopes from the past,
There nothing is normal, nothing outcast.

I know a place,
Where right conquers wrong,
I know a place,
Where the people are strong,
They laugh, sing and dance to music that's played,
Thanking each other that life has been made.

I know a place,
Where the dream starts to fade,
I know a place,
Where the people aren't paid,
The fresh waters flowing, start to dry up,
There's not enough friendship to fill everyone's cup.

I know a place,
That is changing too fast,
I know a place,
Where the beauty won't last,
The place that I loved, is slipping away,
And the people still there, are all left to pay.

Think Global

I know a place,
Where the silence grows loud,
I know a place,
Where the people aren't proud,
When the fairytales fade, and it's all one big lie,
The people stop believing, and all choose to die.

I know a place,
That can start again,
I know a place,
That can forget about pain,
It only takes one, to listen and hope,
That one can teach others to care and to cope.

I know a place,
That almost disappeared,
I know a place,
That the people feared,
But the tears that were shed, formed an oasis,
That's why there's always hope for saving places.

Katriona Fogden (15)

Think Global

The Threatened Land

Underfoot grows no more grass,
Black and dead, this forest that I pass,
Only the polluted air left, on which to gasp,
And the traffic hurtling past.

Yet I remember well when on childish ramble,
The grassy glade, the tree to climb, the scratchy bramble,
Once I'd seen wild bird, fox and rabbit run in a cool, leafy place,
Now all that's left is this terrible symbol of our disgrace.

Here once stood mighty, leafy trees,
Cliffs were once washed by the clean sea breeze,
Fox and deer once ran free,
The pollution that killed them, is now killing me.

"Why not reverse the trend?" I hear you ask,
"That would cost money!" politicians gasp,
"No, we will just live for today,
Why worry? Tomorrow someone else will pay."

And when all the world is dead,
The land and sea burned red,
Even Death will cry for the bleeding land,
That he will hold beneath his withered hand.

Aisa Brooker (14)

Bricks and Mortar

Little Moreton Hall

I don't remember much
When I was born in 1450
But when people made me bigger
I remember more.

Ralph Moreton started building me
And William helped me too
They lived in me and loved me
For 600 years
Then farmers came and used me
But the Moretons watched me still.

The years went by so fast
People came and went
Sometimes children,
Sometimes grown ups.
Life was very sad when people went to war
The people cried and so did I
Though silently because houses aren't meant to cry.

My walls started to crumble
My windows broke
I seemed to go to sleep
Then I sprang alive again
As people came and helped me
They bandaged my wounds and sores
Now I'm whole again
Happy because people visit me.
The best time every year,
Is when people come and watch Shakespeare plays
It reminds me of my childhood.

Sarah Hunt (8)

The House

Dense woods of golden bracken hide the house,
Countless years have passed
Since human life was here.
Spiders stretch walls in the hall and wait,
Owls have made their home,
Bats colonise the rafters
And the noise of mice is everywhere.
Floorboards creak with age and pain,
Windows cracked, covered with dust,
Shredded velvet curtains, worn carpet on the stairs,
In cupboards, faded photos,
On shelves, books with age-stained pages mark time.

Time has passed,
Feet crunch the Autumn carpet in the porch,
Voices murmur, hinges groan,
Through opened windows sunlight rains,
Cool air disturbs the dust.
A workman's whistle echoes through the house,
Ladders rattle, tools clatter,
Smells of rich paint hang heavy in the air.
The furniture moves in, the ghosts move out.
To gardens full of birdsong
The doors are opened wide.

Lauren Coffey (12)

Bricks and Mortar

Chartwell

Pictures on the wall,
A patterned rug on the floor,
Scissors resting on the desk,
Paint brushes bathing in a jug,
An easel and overall waiting for a canvas,
An umbrella hanging upside down like a bat,
A pile of logs waiting to be burnt.

Outside, the thirty two kinds
Of golden roses
And the big red wall
He built himself.

Edward Goodacre (8)*

The Albert Street Cutting

The Albert Street Cutting,
    by the Bridgewater Canal,
        rotten, wooden buttresses,
            spooky, quiet echoes.

Wide and tall,
    long, like a tunnel,
        still and quiet.

Interesting and historic,
    dating to Victorian Times,
        I would like it saved.

Jacob Churchill (10)

Bricks and Mortar

Fieldwalking

*(the recently discovered site of a Roman
Villa in Tockenham village)*

My eyes dance from edge to edge
Scanning,

The ploughed field, heaps of earth
Mounds like hills, hide small clues,

My eyes glance from edge to edge
Sweeping.

I walk the ghost of the Roman villa
Where shadows mark the vanished walls,
My hands sweaty and stained with dirt,
I pick at grey, blue and terracotta
Stuff my pockets with history's broken pieces.

Sifting through,
I catch a signal
As the sun flashes like an S.O.S
From a hand held mirror,
MAYDAY!
A fallen plane, a sinking ship
The last survivor clinging to the wreck,
A bright thing digs its way out
From beneath the collapse of centuries.

I turn it to the light,
A stone cat's claw sits in my palm,
A flint scraper
Sharp edged
To scour fat from skins
Which hung in caves, long before the Romans arrived
To build their roads.

Bricks and Mortar

This flint confronts me,
Prehistory sits in my palm
This, the oldest tool working before the Romans
And is still sharp,
It cuts this paper, these words.

*Katie-Ellen McCrory (12)**

If you find any remains from the past lying on the ground when out walking, you should make a note of where you found them and take them (in the state in which they were found) to your local museum to find out more.

Country Mansion

I remember people, their voices like silvery bells,
ringing,
Ghostly, rising, falling, echoing through me.

They were my people,
And they created me, and they lived in me,
And they were a part of me.

I remember drifts of music, solitary notes,
Floating into my walls, resounding in my corridors,
Like smoke in an autumn bonfire
Fading into silence.

And I remember the cold time, when everything was white,
And I fell into a frost-nipped haze
Of drowsiness.

I remember the gardens where everything was green,
And there was an earthy, leafy, moist smell,
And everything was growing.

Then I was alone.

I was in a time
Where everything
Had gone.
And I was struggling
Against a new world
It was slowly
Pushing me
Into a
Silent
Space
Of loneliness

Bricks and Mortar

But, somewhere, somebody felt me, And they came to me,
And they brought more voices,
Until I was Ringing, Ringing with feeling, and voices,
And I didn't need to remember any more.

Rosemary Griffith (14)

Bricks and Mortar

Saving Places

I see a child,
Laughing,
In my dreams.
Oh, innocent me.
Pure marble skin
and
satin curls
spread out on pillow sheets.

I see an old woman,
Struggling,
Through my eyes.
Knows everything
the child didn't,
Sees everything
the child couldn't.

I see a house
upon the rocks.
Holds memories of
past.
Grips moments with
death.

Children –
Save the house
upon the rocks.
Save the heart
beyond the woman.

Jacqueline Macalesher (16)

Doctor of Castles

Castle of Bodiam is ruined.
Graffiti covers the walls,
People hack out holes any day.
But then comes the doctor of castles,
Graffiti disappears,
Safety rails are put by stairs,
And bones of prisoners who were never released are buried.
But the doctor carries on working,
His work is not over yet,
The beautiful, natural coastline is covered with human waste.
Five hundred and fifty miles of coastline is saved,
Five hundred and ninety thousand acres of countryside,
Three hundred historic houses, and
One hundred and fifty gardens are owned by
Doctor of castles,
Doctor of coastline,
Doctor of countryside,
Doctor of historic houses,
And Doctor of gardens.

Brigid Jones (8)

The House

The crumbling turret of sandy red brick.
The moss sown by the hands of time.
Spears of black railings, rusty and ruined.
Ghostly ragged curtains blowing at gaping windows,
But there are familiar smells and sounds of home.

Then blue flashes of uniform,
And artificial echoing sounds of strangers.
A grip clamped my arm through the vacuum
A glance at the petrified blurred faces,
My rotting home fluttered before my eyes.

The whirring of machine ceased,
Hard, emotionless voices shrieked.
The icy chain dented my flesh.
The room gave into tremors and violent shakes.
But our family would stick together – whatever the
   world threw at us.

Our hands, the only contact with each other,
Looped through the mouldering wall – bulging with
   despair.
My hair, now a knotted tangle of weeds, grew into the
   wall and fixed there.

Such happy memories of warmth and hope.
Somewhere to belong – not special, but our one right.
Now risking our future to save the four rooms,
Our safety, our comfort –
And our home.

Fritha Waters (14)

A Living Heritage

Saving places is not like collecting butterflies.
So many deathly splendours under glass.
It is re-living lingering laughter, longing sighs;
Safe-guarding burnished memories of what's passed.
If we merely grasp the whirling dust of history,
We neglect the real lives of ancient realms.
The captivating spell, the tick-tock mystery,
The dragon dreads of pioneering helms.
Beside our hoard of mortal change, a cache of constants,
Will keep our fleeting lives in place within the frame.
The slumbering hills, eternal sky and sea's persistence.
All show introverted demons as our shame.
Today we climb the tree of time, and glimpse the deep-thrown roots,
It is up to us to tend the oak and nourish next spring's shoots.

Louise Marr (17)

Saving Places

Well trodden flags
Majestic curving arches
Stairways hand polished
Chiselled stonework

Rooms to let
Mine to rent
Jug n Basin share
Rare wallpaper care

Overflowing lawns carry
Trees dipping branches
Red deer vistas
Quiet, timeless, patient

Laundries – court enclosed
Toil long settled
Byres stretched, now
Coca Cola's stand

Perambulator nanny pushed
Past sapling young
Dappling oaks o'er
Lap tops brood

People in	People out
Take a little	Lose a lot
Save a little	Keep a lot
My heritage	Your trust

Tracey Holland (13)

Grandma's Book

"Take out the photo album", Grandma said,
As on Saturday night, the rain, trickled down the window pane
And I sat on her knee drinking sweet milk tea
As she shared her long preserved memories with me.

Old Hatcher's wood leapt from the page
Yellowed, slightly torn and marked with age
And she reminisced of nature walks,
Long forgotten tree houses and girly talks,
Hide and seek among towering Oak trees,
Foraging for Dock leaves to ease nettle-stung knees.

The country parks, wide open land
Where couples walked hand in hand,
Where Grandma said goodbye to her love
As shadows were cast by kamikaze planes above.

Sticks of rock and daisy chains,
Four leaf clovers,
Model aeroplanes.
Scrap-books heavy with picture postcards
Celebration streamers stretching for yards.

Then Grandma closed the heavy book
And tucked it back in its little nook.
She closed her eyes and let out a sigh
And then I said my last goodbye.

Today I walked in Hatcher's wood
And my children came along.
We played, we laughed and sat in the sun
And listened to the lark's song.

The memories trapped in Grandma's book
Now are hidden by layers of dust.
The places she loved stand tall today
Under the watchful care of the National Trust.

Elizabeth Nolan (15)

Saving Places

To saunter, for ever, along the coast
With its stones glinting like bleached bones,
For ever, for everyone.
To enjoy, for ever, the sight of puffins,
Perched on the cliff top.
For ever, for everyone.

To walk, for ever, across the deserted moorland.
For ever, for everyone.
To see, for ever, the ponies
Grazing in the heather.
For ever, for everyone.

To stroll, for ever, through sun-shot woodlands.
For ever, for everyone.
To be surprised, for ever, at a glimpse
Of a red squirrel peering through the branches.
For ever, for everyone.

Jessica Goodacre (10)

The Rescue

There's a house in the distance –
A big one too,
A few can go inside it –
But not me or you.

The ones who go inside it
From the National Trust
Go to mend it and repair it
And to give it a good dust.

They're tidying the bedrooms,
They're working on the floor,
They're cleaning all the windows,
They're varnishing the door.

They're shining up the silver,
They're polishing the brass,
And outside in the garden,
Is someone cutting grass.

They're planting all the seedlings,
And pretty flowers too,
And lots of little saplings
Of oak and ash and yew.

They've done the restoration
And now it's good as new –
And all can go inside it
Including me and you.

Fiona Biddington (9)

Saving Places

I went to Witley Common with my Mum,
I turned a tree into my home.
We met people walking dogs,
We enjoyed jumping over logs.
   I wonder, when I'm old and grey,
   Will the National Trust treasure
   The walks I go on today?

I went to Mottisfont and met my Aunt,
We had a picnic on the grass.
We loved the rose garden, and the river too,
There was so much to see and do.
   I wonder when I'm old and grey,
   Will the National Trust treasure
   The gardens I enjoy today?

I went to Sudbury with my Gran,
I took a teddy round with me.
We saw how children used to work and play
When Gran was a girl in the olden days.
   I wonder, when I'm old and grey,
   Will the National Trust treasure
   The games I play with today?

I went to Petworth with a friend,
We listened to a concert and didn't want it to end.
We took teddies to throw in the air,
Don't you wish that you were there?
   I wonder, when I'm old and grey,
   Will the National Trust treasure
   The music I listen to today?

I'm sure that when I'm old and grey,
The National Trust will treasure things
Like it does today.
The National Trust – for ever, for everyone.

Ruth Spiers (8)

Trust Us

The Animals Speak

"Forever" chattered the red squirrel in the dense Langdale forest,
"Forever" croaked the natterjack toad as he crawled along Cock Marsh,
"Forever" squawked the puffins as they perched on the rocks at crumbling Dunwich,
"Forever" swooped the bat as he listened to the plainsong at Fountains Abbey,
"Forever" neighed the ponies as they grazed on the lush grass of Dartmoor,
"Forever" chorused the barn owls in the tall trees of Osterley Park,
"Forever" chanted the otters as they swam on the West Bank of the Avon,
"Forever" squeaked the dormice as they scuttled through the attics of Calke Abbey,
"Forever" trumpeted the seals on the slippery rocks of the Farne Islands,
"Forever, for everyone".

Melissa Dawes (12)

Index

*Winners

Anderson, Kelly	Hardley School, Hampshire	34
Bagshaw, Katy	Kyle Academy, Ayrshire	12
Barlow, Alissa	Newlands School, Berkshire	25
Benfield, Jo	Wymondham College, Norfolk	37
Berkson, Sarah	The Perse School, Cambridgeshire	13
Biddington, Fiona	St. John's Primary School, Staffordshire	60
Bourne, Hugo	Shocklach Oviatt C. E. Primary, Cheshire	17
Brooker, Aisa	Woodford County High School, Essex	45
Cam, Sarah	Woolston County Primary, Cheshire	23
Camplin, May	Halesworth Middle School, Suffolk	24
Chilvers, Cassandra	Combs Ford County Primary, Suffolk	36
Churchill, Jacob	Northmoor Green County Primary, Somerset	48
Coffey, Lauren	Northgate High School, Suffolk	47
Craven, Kim	Halesworth Middle School, Suffolk	11
*Dawes, Melissa	Kell Bank C of E School, North Yorkshire	62
Eley, Katherine	Enfield County L. W. School, Middlesex	22
*Evans, Llywelyn	Y Coleg Llanymddyfri, Dyfed	19
Fogden, Katriona	Trinity School, Cumbria	43
Frige, Luciano	St. Thomas' Primary School, Kent	32
Gilbert, Eleanor	Shocklach Oviatt C. E. Primary, Cheshire	27
*Goodacre, Edward	Kell Bank C of E School, North Yorkshire	48
Goodacre, Jessica	Kell Bank C of E School, North Yorkshire	59
*Goss, Robert	Halesworth Middle School, Suffolk	14
Graham, Sarah	Woodfield Avenue Junior School, West Midlands	29
Grant, Rhys	Combs Ford County Primary, Suffolk	15
Griffith, Rosemary	Educated at home in East Sussex	51
Holland, Tracey	St. Patrick's Girls Academy, County Tyrone	57
Hunt, Sarah	The Groves School, Staffordshire	46

Index

Jones, Brigid	Stafford Junior School, East Sussex	54
Jones, Katharine	Chickerell County Primary, Dorset	30
***Jones**, Rachel	Chickerell County Primary, Dorset	07
Knight, Bethany	Headlands County Primary, York	16
Landau, Christopher	Monmouth School, Gwent	35
Macalesher, Jacqueline	Clevedon School, Avon	53
Marr, Louise	Graham School, North Yorkshire	56
***McCrory**, Katie-Ellen	South Wiltshire Grammar School, Wiltshire	49
***McKeown**, Ciara	St. Columbas School, Clydebank	42
***Mills**, Sophie	Malvern Girls College, Worcestershire	33
Moore, Gillian	Halfway County Primary, Dyfed	31
Murphy, Cecilia	St. Christopher's School, London	41
Nolan, Elizabeth	West Kirby Grammar School for Girls, Merseyside	58
O'Rourke, Thomas	Shimna Integrated College, Co. Down	21
Rowe, Rueben	St. Gregory's R.C. High School, Cheshire	08
Rowley, Gavin	Mead Vale Primary School, Avon	18
Sillett, Sarah	Combs Ford County Primary, Suffolk	21
Sims, Johnnie	Combs Ford County Primary, Suffolk	09
Spiers, Ruth	Churcher's College Junior School, Hampshire	61
Stanborough, Adam	Halesworth Middle School, Suffolk	28
Stockton, Louise	All Saints C.E.V.A Primary School, Suffolk	27
Thomas, Henry	Halesworth Middle School, Suffolk	39
Tobin, Hannah	South Hampstead High School, London	38
Waters, Fritha	Sir John Leman High School, Suffolk	55
***White**, Keren	Highworth Grammar School for Girls, Kent	10
Whitford, Nina	Clitheroe Royal Grammar School, Lancs	40
***Winterbourne**, James	Shocklach Oviatt C. E. Primary, Cheshire	06